BABY BOY, WHAT WILL YOU BE?

Written by Terquoia Bourne
Art by Jerry Craft

MAMA'S BOYZ, INC • NORWALK

BABY BOY, WHAT WILL YOU BE?

Written by Terquoia Bourne
Illustrated by Jerry Craft
Edited by Ernestine Eisenhauer
Title design by Danni Ai

Summary: On a cold winter day, a new mom snuggles with her baby boy and warms her heart with the thoughts of all the limitless possibilities that he can achieve.

Follow on Twitter
Terquoia Bourne @thepenmommy
Jerry Craft @JerryCraft

ISBN-13: 978-1-7323184-1-0

First Edition
Printed in the United States

Published by Mama's Boyz, Inc. (www.jerrycraft.com)

Thank You

To Jamal: Thank you for believing in me and embracing my dream.

To Mom and Dad: I never stopped writing, the words were just hiding in my heart, yearning for a voice. Thank you for recognizing the gift in me, that I had yet to recognize in myself.

To Judah and Mycah: Thank you for constantly reminding me of my purpose. Always remember to DREAM BIG!

To Aunt Gwen: Your support has been endless. Thank you for cheering me on to the finish line.

To Aunt Laura: Thank you for your prayers and encouragement.

To Andrea, Aunt Zeida, Candi, Carmen, Danyelle, Jamiela, Mary, Ms. Olivia, Paulette and Yashica: Each of you have made a meaningful impact during my journey to becoming an author.

To Jerry Craft: Thank you for helping to make my dream of publishing my first book become a reality.

My precious baby boy,
you're such a sight to behold.
I will always be your biggest
fan, even when I'm gray
and old.

When I gaze upon your face,
there's so much hope I see.
As I gaze, I begin to wonder
just what you'll grow up and be.

Baby boy, sweet baby boy, what will you be?

Will you be an *Astronaut* in a space shuttle that soars up high?

Or will you be an *Architect* who makes buildings that touch the sky?

Maybe you will be a *Scientist* who studies plants and seeds.

Perhaps you will be a
Community Helper
who loves to do good deeds.

You might be a **Deep Sea Diver** who swims where fish play.

How about a *Daddy*
who cares for his little ones,
while mommy works each day?

Baby boy, sweet baby boy, what will you be?

Will you be a caring **Doctor**
who makes sick people feel better?

Or will you be a devoted *School Teacher*
who helps children learn numbers and letters?

Maybe you will be a *Pastry Chef* who bakes yummy cakes and sweets.

Baby boy, sweet baby boy,
what will you be?

My love and good wishes are
beyond the moon for you,
so every night I say a prayer
that all your dreams come true.

In life there will be challenges,
but I know you were born to fly.
As you grow older, one day you'll see
that the best cure for fear is to try.

Give it your all, do your best,
and the world will be yours to see.

Have a bit of faith,
believe in yourself,
and there's **nothing**
you can't be!

While you're making Mommy proud, remember to enjoy life's adventure.

But for now,
just be my baby,
resting in my arms,
on this peaceful
night in winter.

Good night, my
beautiful boy.

Dream Big.

TERQUOIA BOURNE

photo credit: Glenn Pictures

photo credit: Glenn Pictures

Author: Terquoia Bourne is an early-childhood educator, wife and mother of two beautiful children. She is an Oregon native, but spent most of her childhood in northern California. Growing up, Terquoia's parents taught her and her younger brother the importance of making a positive impact in the lives of others and the community. This life lesson inspired Terquoia to pursue a career that enabled her to nurture and educate young children.

Terquoia is proud alumna of California State University Long Beach. She earned her Bachelor of Arts in Child Development and Family Studies in 2005. She later returned to school to complete her Master's Degree in Early Childhood Education in 2013. Terquoia describes herself as "a complex person, with many layers." However, beneath all those layers is simply a sincere soul who loves God and her family, and is determined to live in her purpose.

For more info email her at themommybehindthepen@gmail.com.

JERRY CRAFT

photo credit: Hollis King

Illustrator: Jerry Craft has illustrated and written close to three dozen children's books, including his acclaimed anti-bullying book, "The Offenders: Saving the World While Serving Detention!" In 2014, Jerry illustrated "The Zero Degree Zombie Zone," for Scholastic which earned him recognition from the Junior Library Guild. He is the creator of Mama's Boyz, an award-winning comic strip that was distributed by King Features Syndicate from 1995-2013. Jerry has won five African American Literary Awards. He is also a co-founder and co-producer of the *Schomburg's Annual Black Comic Book Festival* which draws more than 10,000 fans each year. Look for his middle grade graphic novel "New Kid," which will be published by HarperCollins in February 2019. For more info, email him at jerrycraft@aol.com, or visit www.jerrycraft.com

CPSIA information can be obtained
at www.ICGtesting.com
Printed in the USA
LVHW071526040419
612997LV00018B/1013/P

9 781732 318410